Our Christmas Story

Our Christmas Story
by Mrs. Billy Graham

as told to
Elizabeth Sherrill

Illustrations by David Koechel

Decision Books

World Wide Publications ∘ Minneapolis, Minnesota

ACKNOWLEDGEMENTS

Scripture quotations taken from The Living Bible, copyright © 1971,
by Tyndale House Publishers, Wheaton, Illinois 60187.
Used by permission.

OUR CHRISTMAS STORY. Copyright © 1959, by Elizabeth Sherrill.
Illustrations copyright © 1973, by World Wide Publications,
Minneapolis, Minnesota.
All rights reserved. Published by World Wide Publications,
1313 Hennepin Avenue, Minneapolis, Minnesota 55403.

Library of Congress Catalog Number 73-84958.

Printed in the U.S.A.

Foreword

When it was suggested that Ruth tell the
Christmas story for children everywhere, we
were delighted. But we had to warn the publisher
that "our" Christmas story would be different from
the traditional manger scene that spells Christmas
for many people.

Of course, the manger scene is an important
part of Christmas in our home — the joyous and
beloved climax to the story. But it is only a part
of the story. For Christmas does not begin in the
stable of Bethlehem. It does not begin in the
Gospel of Luke, but in the Book of Genesis.

Visitors to our home at Christmas are sometimes
startled when I read the tragic story from the Old
Testament before an evening of carols.

"Aren't these grim thoughts for this happy time
of year?" they ask. "The season of Jesus's birth

is no time to talk of death. What do Adam and Eve have to do with Christmas?"

To which we answer: Everything. Without the story of sin in the Old Testament, what can the good news of the New Testament say? Without sin, we have no need of a Savior. We cannot separate our joy at Christ's coming from our desperate need for Him. Unless we have witnessed the tragedy of man's separation from God through the millennia before Bethlehem, then the birth of a baby in a stable is just that for us, no more.

Nor can we separate His birth from the work He came to earth to do. Without His death, His birth has no meaning. The birth without the Cross is a gift half-given. Many would rather not think of the Cross at Christmastime. They take the angels' song, but reject all that it implies. In doing this, they rob themselves of the full joy of Christmas.

Children are more realistic than adults. They have no trouble in grasping the real meaning of good and evil in a story. In this respect, we need to be more like children. When we see Christmas not as a sentimental, isolated event, but as the focal point in human history, it becomes a day of rejoicing indeed.

Here, of course, that history must be simplified and abbreviated. No one is more aware than Ruth of what her book leaves out and what it does not say. It is not a theological treatise, but a book for children. Ruth has tried to hint at the riches of the Bible, not to provide an inventory of them. Her hope is that this approach to Christmas will lead the readers of this book to the Bible itself for the full story in all its wonder.

Ruth and I believe that it has never been more important than it is today for children to read and love the Bible. In this age of "go with the crowd," boys and girls can take courage from its lonely giants — men like Noah and Moses — who, as Ruth expresses it, closed their ears to the many in order to listen to the One.

If this little book helps children to see in the whole Bible the glorious meaning of Christ's coming, Ruth's prayers — and mine — for it will be abundantly answered.

Billy Graham

Contents

Christmas at Our House

*My mother always
served oyster stew for
Christmas breakfast
when I was a girl
in China. It was a
family custom.*

Christmas at Our House

o you ever have oysters for breakfast?

We do, once a year, on Christmas morning.

Perhaps you wonder why we have them then. When I go to the grocery store the day before Christmas and ask for oysters, I like to tell the man when I'm going to serve them.

"Oysters for breakfast!" he says, and he is very puzzled. Then I explain that my mother always served oyster stew for Christmas breakfast when I was a girl in China. It was a family custom. And when my father, who is a doctor, decided that it was time to bring his family back to America we brought back the custom of oysters for Christmas breakfast, too.

Let's pretend that you've come to visit us on Christmas. There's a special reason why it has to be Christmas, of all the days in the year. This is the day when, after all the presents are opened, we sit in front of the fire and hear the Christmas story from the Bible. I want you to pretend that you're hearing it with us because, later, I want to ask you a question about it.

Of course, your own parents can't really spare you for Christmas. Christmas is one of those days when parents want their families at home. This will be just a pretend visit — and that will have one advantage: you'll only have to eat pretend oysters.

I'll tell you about our house so that you can imagine you are here. In the first place, there are our dogs. One is a Great Pyrenees. His name is Belshazzar because in Old Testament times there was a king named Belshazzar who gave a great feast for a thousand lords, and every time we see Belshazzar eat we feel as though we're feeding a thousand lords, too. He's so big you can ride on his back. Our children do, so there's no reason why you can't.*

Our house will make you think of a pioneer's cabin off in the woods. We asked the men who built it to leave the logs showing and the walls rough, like those of an old-fashioned log cabin. It's just the place to run and make things and play with the dogs and not worry

*Belshazzar is no longer with us but has been replaced by other pets.

14

about the furniture.

And if you like to do things with people your own age, I'm sure you'll like it up here. We have five children of our own and at Christmastime there is always a bunch of cousins, too. Our own children are:

Gigi (she's the oldest, and her real name isn't Gigi — it's Virginia)

Ann (who has such a short name we couldn't make it any shorter)

Bunny (Bunny's real name is Ruth, like mine)

Franklin (whose real name is Franklin)

Ned ("Ned" is short — very short — for Nelson Edman)

So you'll be certain to find someone your own age to do things with, up here.**

When I say "up here," I mean up on a mountain. Our house is almost at the top, with a very steep road leading up to it. There are lots of places to explore. You might try the cave down the hill, or the orchard behind the house where the bears come. Don't worry about the bears; they are sleeping at Christmastime. Besides, the dogs are bound to be tagging along behind you, and they're so big they'd give any bear quite a scare.

But now let's say that it's Christmas morning. The tree is over there by the window, with the presents

**The Graham children are grown up now and have their own little families.

15

beneath it and its branches loaded down with warm-colored lights, candy canes, ornaments, and the smallest gifts. And here in front of the enormous fireplace — big enough to stand up in, when there's no fire — are the stockings, one for every child and cousin and, of course, one for you. The presents have to wait until after breakfast, but the stockings are for now.

After the stockings comes breakfast, and you know what is on the table today, don't you? Oysters, floating in a big, steaming stew. (Want to know a secret? Personally, I don't like oysters for breakfast. I never did, not even when I was a girl, about your age, back in China. But the stew part is fine.)

Our children think breakfast takes forever on Christmas morning. Never do the grown-ups eat so much. They sit around and drink cup after cup of coffee, and they lean back and talk about how long it's been since they were all together, and they even waste precious minutes looking out over the valley and saying what a lovely day it is. But then comes the wonderful moment when finally they're through, and they get up, scraping their chairs on the floor, and everyone goes back into the living room to open the presents.

It takes a long time because everyone wants to see what everyone else has received. But finally the very last package is opened. The floor is a heap of paper

and ribbons and the grown-ups are saying, as they did last year, that there's really too much and that next year they will have to buy fewer presents.

And now comes the moment that's really Christmas. The fire is snapping. Christmas music is playing softly on the record player. Everyone makes himself comfortable, some on the floor, some in chairs, some on the window seat. It's time for the Christmas story. Father opens the Bible to the second chapter of the Book of Luke. When he begins to read the room is suddenly still with a special stillness that it has only at this time on Christmas morning. We are very quiet as we listen again to the wonderful story:

About this time Caesar Augustus, the Roman Emperor, decreed that a census should be taken throughout the nation....Everyone was required to return to his ancestral home for this registration. And because Joseph was a member of the royal line, he had to go to Bethlehem in Judea, King David's ancient home — journeying there from the Galilean village of Nazareth. He took with him Mary, his fiancee, who was obviously expecting a child by this time. And while they were there, the time came for her baby to be born; and she gave birth to her first child, a son. She wrapped him in a blanket and laid him in a manger, because there was no room for them in the village inn. That night some shepherds were in the fields outside the village, guarding their flocks of sheep. Suddenly an angel appeared among them,..."Don't be afraid!" he said. "I bring you the most joyful news ever announced, and it is for everyone! The Savior — yes, the Messiah, the Lord — has been born tonight in Bethlehem!"

The fire is burning low. The cat is purring. Outside, perhaps it has begun to snow. The special quiet that the Christmas story brings has filled the whole room.

Now here is the question I wanted to ask you: Is this the very beginning of the Christmas story? Or does it sound as though we had started right in the middle of it? The angel called this Baby a Savior — someone who saves. If you fell through the ice when you were skating and a man rushed up to pull you from the water, that man would be your savior. But if this Baby was a Savior, what was he to save us from? It sounds as if there were a lot more to the story.

What is the whole Christmas story? It's really much too long to tell now, when we have all the ribbons and boxes to pick up and Christmas dinner to fix. Besides, the best stories aren't told all at once. They're told little by little, as we dry the dishes or get ready for bed. Bedtime is really the best time for storytelling.

There's only one thing to do. We'll just have to pretend that you're spending the whole week with us. Then every night, at bedtime, I can tell you a little more of the Christmas story, starting from the very beginning.

We'll imagine you are sleeping in the guest room. There's the biggest bed in there you ever saw — an old-fashioned press bed, higher than your head. In fact, another bed fits underneath it. That other bed is called a trundle bed because it "trundles" out from under the big one. Maybe you'd rather sleep in the trundle bed — if anyone ever fell out of the high one he'd hit awfully hard!

When story time comes each evening, we'll gather all the children that are around and we'll pile onto the bed with you and listen. I've told them the story dozens of times, but they never get tired of hearing it.

In the Beginning

In the Beginning

*I*f the Book of Luke gives us only part of the Christmas story, where is the rest of it?

To find the beginning of the story, we have to go back a long way. The first Christmas when Jesus was born in Bethlehem was almost two thousand years ago, but we have to go back farther than that. We have to go back before Mary and Joseph themselves were born. Back before there was any town of Bethlehem. Before there were any towns at all. Even before there were any people on the earth. In fact, so far back that there was no earth.

There were no stars then either. No sun, no sky, no rain. In those days — except that there were no

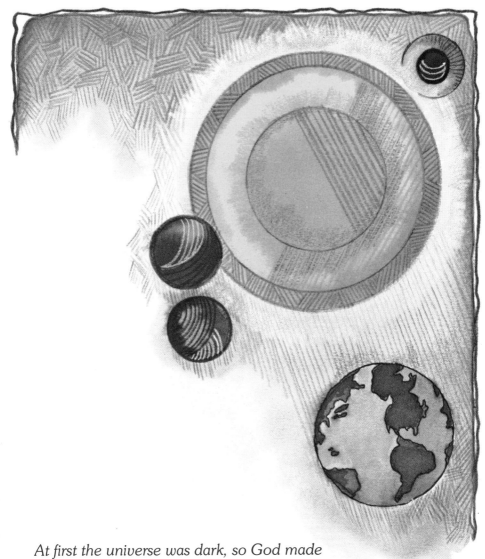

At first the universe was dark, so God made the burning stars — our sun among them — for light. He made our earth and then He filled it with wonders.

days — space was empty. In all the universe, there was only God Himself — and the angels.

The Christmas story goes back that far.

In that long ago, unimaginable time, God began to make things. He made things because He was God, and God loves to make things.

At first the universe was dark, so God made the burning stars — our sun among them — for light. He made our earth and then He filled it with wonders. He put deep oceans and high mountains on it. In the oceans He put octopuses and giant fish and creatures so tiny that only He could see them. On the mountains He put goats, and He made them wonderful climbers. In the valleys He put all sorts of animals — caterpillars and parrots and rhinoceroses. And of course, He made oysters! He made billions and trillions of creatures and not one was exactly like another.

God loved the things He had made. He loved His raindrops and His octopuses and His daylight. But He had no children to share them with Him. In all the earth, there was no one like Himself, no one to say, "How beautiful it is!" And no one to enjoy it with Him.

In the whole earth, no one to have a conversation with! God talked to His creation, of course. He talked to His flowers with His warm sunshine and His cool rain. In every little fish egg He put a message, telling that egg how to grow into a fish instead of a rhinoceros. And all of His creatures obeyed Him, but not one of them answered Him.

To have a companion on earth, God needed someone like Himself. So He made one more creature. He made our kind of creature and He made it in His own image. That is, He copied us after Himself.

He made two of us, a man and a woman. The man's name was Adam and the woman's name was Eve. As soon as He had made them, God loved them more than all the other creatures He had made. He wanted to shower them with gifts. He gave them all His cows and His fish and His bees — yes, and His oysters, too. Every animal on the whole earth and in all the oceans he gave to Adam and Eve. He gave them all His trees and plants. From the tallest date palm to the flattest mushroom, they were all for Adam and Eve.

Then He found the most beautiful spot on earth for them to live in. It was named Eden and it was so beautiful it was called a garden. In the Garden of Eden God put everything that Adam and Eve needed to make them happy. There were rivers of clear water to drink, fruit to eat, vines to swing on, flowers to smell.

They didn't need spears, or any kind of weapon,

He gave them all His trees and plants. From the tallest date palm to the flattest mushroom, they were all for Adam and Eve.

because they had no enemies. There were no wild animals in those days either. Lions and bears and hyenas came when Adam called them and lay down on the ground to be played with, because they knew they belonged to him. Adam loved the animals and they loved him.

Adam and Eve didn't need a house to live in or warm clothes to wear because it was never cold in Eden, and God kept the wind and the rain off of them. They didn't need a stove or a refrigerator or even pans to cook with, since all the food they wanted grew on the trees for them. And they certainly didn't need money, since God had already given them everything.

God watched the two people He had made, and He loved them. He was delighted when Eve picked the flowers and gave them pretty names and put them in her hair. "She loves My flowers!" God thought. He liked to see Adam stroke the lions and the buffaloes and call them wonderful and handsome and marvelous. Best of all, He liked to hear Adam and Eve say, "All these things were made by God."

For work, God gave them the care of His beautiful garden. Adam and Eve loved their work. All morning they pruned the trees and dug the earth until it was soft around the flowers. Then, when their work was finished, they would run with the antelope, swim with

God watched the two people He had made, and He loved them. He was delighted when Eve picked the flowers and gave them pretty names and put them in her hair.

the otter, sing with the oriole. Best of all, they would wait for the moment of God's visit.

For God loved Adam and Eve so much that every evening, at the close of the long, happy day, He came into the garden and talked with them. And then — new joy on earth! — the man and the woman answered Him. It was the moment God had waited for since He had created the world.

"At last," He thought, "I have My children with whom I can share the joy and the glory of My creation."

The Testing Tree

The Testing Tree

So far, this has been a happy story because it has been about God's plan for His world — and for us. God's plan was for us to live always in perfect fellowship with Him. In His plan, there was no sickness, no hunger, no war, no unhappiness. We were to be His companions, to live closer to Him than His other creatures.

But wait. Are we living the happy life God planned? Has anyone you know ever been sick? Do people fight wars? Do you ever quarrel with your brothers and sisters? Is there unhappiness in the world? Something must have gone wrong with God's plan.

Something did go wrong, and the something was

this: the people whom God had made did not follow His plan.

But, you say, He was God! Why didn't He *make* them follow it?

But there, you see, was the difference between the animals God had made and these new creatures called humans. Animals *must* follow God's plan for them; they have no choice. A caterpillar does not say to himself, "Let's see, shall I spin myself a cocoon and turn into a butterfly, or is it more fun just to be a caterpillar?" He spins a cocoon because he cannot help it.

But from human beings, God wanted something more than blind, unthinking obedience. He wanted Adam and Eve to follow His plan not because they had to, but because they wanted to. He wanted them to join Him willingly, eagerly in fellowship rather than mechanical agreement. He wanted them to be people rather than robots. And so, to man alone, God gave the power of choice.

It was a bold experiment, because there was the terrible possibility that this new creature might choose *not* to follow God's plan. That was the risk God took when He made Adam and Eve. But, in His love God took that risk.

In the very center of the Garden of Eden was a tall and beautiful tree on which grew a strange and lovely

In the very center of the Garden of Eden was a tall and beautiful tree on which grew a strange and lovely fruit.

fruit. But beautiful though it was, this tree was forbidden to Adam and Eve.

"If you eat its fruit, you will be doomed to die," God had said.

This was the testing tree, to see whether Adam and Eve would choose to follow God's plan. "Surely," thought God, "it is an easy test, when there are hundreds of trees in the garden whose fruit they may eat. After all I have done for them, surely they will do this much for Me."

Here is where sorrow enters the story. For Adam and Eve, instead of listening to God who had made them, listened to the words of someone who hated them.

One day a snake who lived in the garden came up to Eve.

"Really?" asked the snake in his skeptical voice. *"None of the fruit in the garden? God says you mustn't eat any of it?"*

"Of course we may eat it," said Eve. *"It's only the fruit from the tree at the center of the garden that we are not to eat. God says we mustn't eat it or even touch it, or we will die."*

The snake laughed a secret laugh. "Are you sure He said that?" he hissed. *"You'll not die! God knows very well that the instant you eat it you will become like Him, for your eyes will be opened — you will be able to tell good from evil!* It will make you wise! As wise as God! Eat it," he whispered, "and you will know everything that He knows!"

Now this snake, as you have already guessed, was no ordinary animal. This was Satan himself. Once, long, long before, Satan had been an angel living with God in heaven. But he was so proud of living with God that he began to imagine he was just as good as God — maybe even better! And so God had to send him away. Like a bolt of lightning Satan fell from heaven. Now, in Adam and Eve, he saw a way to get even, a way to spoil God's plan.

To Eve, the snake's words sounded wonderful. To be wise as God! She shut her mind to what God had said about the tree. In fact, she turned her back on God and His plan. She was full of her own plans now.

She ran to the center of the garden and looked up into the branches of the testing tree. There, just above her, ripe and tempting, hung the fruit. She picked one. For a moment she wondered if it would really kill her. She took a tiny bite of it and waited. Nothing happened. She felt as strong as ever and the fruit was so good! She ate it all and then she picked a piece for Adam and took it to him. And Adam ate it.

It was the first evil thing that ever happened on this earth.

Good-bye to the Garden

Good-bye to the Garden

There is a special word for the evil thing that Adam and Eve did. The word is "sin." To sin means to disobey God, to fall short of His goodness. When Adam and Eve ate the fruit that God had told them not to eat, they committed the first sin, so it is sometimes called "the original sin."

At first, Adam and Eve couldn't see that their sin had hurt them at all. They waited, a bit afraid, for God had said, "You will be doomed to die" — but, after all, they were still alive. So they decided that God had not really meant it.

But Adam and Eve did not understand the kind of death God was talking about. That death was threefold. One part of it had happened instantly — their wonderful fellowship with God had already ended. Part of it had just begun — now everything in the world was under a death sentence. All plants and animals and Adam and Eve themselves would grow old and die. Finally, there was the death of being forever separated from God. But already God was planning a way by which His wayward children could return to Him. This dreadful eternal death would be only for those who refused to follow God's way.

This is what God had warned Adam and Eve about. He had said, "If you choose not to obey Me, then you will be cutting yourself off from Me, and this death will follow." Though Adam and Eve did not know it, it had already begun.

They had scarcely swallowed the fruit when a feeling came over them that they had never felt before. The feeling was shame!

At that moment, they heard God's voice in the garden. He had come for His evening visit and He was calling them.

"Adam! Eve!"

Adam and Eve looked at each other in terror. Always before they had run to meet Him, for this was the best moment of the day. But now they were afraid. For the first time, they did not want to be near

God. They wanted to run far away from Him, to put their fingers in their ears, to pretend they didn't hear.

And so they tried to hide from God. They ran behind some trees and waited, hoping that He would go away.

But God waited for these two children of His. When When they did not come, He called to Adam, "Where are you?"

And Adam came out from behind the trees. He was trembling all over, and he said to God, *"I heard you coming and didn't want you to see me naked."*

Now this was not the truth. The real reason Adam hid was that he had disobeyed God and was afraid he'd be punished. But he still hoped God wouldn't find out about the fruit from the testing tree. So he lied to God.

God's voice was sorrowful and He said, *"Who told you you were naked? Have you eaten fruit from the tree I warned you about?"*

Now Adam saw that there was no use in trying to deceive God. But he still thought perhaps God would not be angry at him if he could blame somebody else. So he pointed to Eve and said, *"It was the woman you gave me who brought me some, and I ate it."*

Then God turned to Eve and when He spoke His voice was stern. "Eve," He said, *"How could you do such a thing?"*

No matter how hard Adam worked, the fruit and grain that he grew did not taste as good as the fruit in the Garden of Eden. Thorns and thistles grew up out of the ground and choked what he planted. When he tried to pull these weeds up, they scratched his hands.

Now Eve was frightened and she looked around for someone to blame. "The snake did it!" she said. "He talked me into it! It was his fault."

But God was not impressed by excuses. All three had done wrong. All three had to take the consequences.

God turned first to the snake. *"You shall grovel in the dust as long as you live, crawling along on your belly."* And ever since, snakes have squirmed along the ground.

As for Adam and Eve, they had shut themselves away from the happy life God had planned for them in the Garden of Eden. They were driven into the windy, cold, rainy world outside. Instead of simply reaching up into the trees for their dinner, they had to plant seeds and pull weeds and raise their own food.

And no matter how hard Adam worked, the fruit and grain that he grew did not taste as good as the fruit in the Garden of Eden. Thorns and thistles grew up out of the ground and choked what he planted. When he tried to pull these weeds up, they scratched his hands. Adam wondered where they came from; he had never seen such things in the garden God had planted.

But worst of all, Adam and Eve had separated themselves from God. They could no longer be the very thing they had been created to be in the first place — God's companions on the earth. The warm and constant fellowship with God was broken. They had stepped outside His plan and now they were homeless.

The Man Who Listened

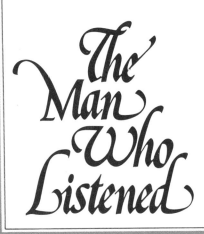

The Man Who Listened

*T*he first sin brought unhappiness to Adam and Eve. But the unhappiness it brought them was nothing compared to the grief it brought God. Here were the creatures He had chosen out of all the universe to be His companions — and they had left Him.

He was lonely again, but now His loneliness was worse than before, because He had had children and then lost them. God, you see, still loved these people He had made. God does not change. No matter how badly they had behaved, they were still His dearest creation.

And so, when they left the Garden, He went with them — with Adam and Eve and their children and

46

their children's children's children — calling them, warning them of danger, trying to teach them. But they wouldn't listen, these children of Adam. Just as Adam and Eve had disobeyed God, so did the people who came after them. Year by year they drifted farther away from God's plan.

Adam and Eve had two sons, Abel and Cain. When they grew up, Cain killed his brother, and that was the first murder. Adam and Eve had more children, and those children had children until there were many people in the world — and most of them were like Cain.

Instead of living together peacefully, they quarreled with each other. The more people a soldier killed in a war, the greater a hero he was. Next to wars, the children of Adam liked noisy pleasures best. In their so-called fun they screamed and shouted and spilled their food like spoiled children, and bragged about how many people they would kill in the next war.

In all the noisy confusion no one heard God calling. No one heard Him say, over and over, that this was not what He had made them for.

At least, very few people heard Him. In every generation there were always one or two who tried hard to shut out the din around them so that they could hear what God was saying.

One of these people was a man called Noah. Noah didn't go to war to kill his neighbors, and he didn't go to the noisy parties. He lived quietly with his wife and three sons, listening all the time for God's message.

Now it happened that God had a very important message for Noah. The Bible tells us:

When the Lord God saw the extent of human wickedness, and that the trend and direction of men's lives were only towards evil, he was sorry he had made them. It broke his heart.

So God decided to wash the whole earth clean with a great rain. But Noah was a good man, and God told him about the flood that was coming. He told Noah to build an ark — a large boat with a house on its deck — big enough to hold his family and some of every kind of animal in the world.

God told Noah exactly how to build it, how long it should be, and how high. *"Construct decks and stalls throughout the ship,"* He said. *"Make three decks inside the boat — a bottom, middle, and upper deck."* He told Noah to put one door and one window in the ark.

Of course, when Noah's loud-mouthed neighbors, who were sitting around wondering what new trouble they could stir up, heard all the hammering at Noah's house, they rushed over to see what old Noah was up to.

When the last chipmunk and caterpillar were in the ark God Himself shut them in.

"He's always got some crazy notion," one man shouted.

"Thinks he hears 'God' talking!" shrieked another. "As if there was any such thing as 'God'!"

When they got there and found Noah building a huge boat on dry land, miles and miles from the ocean, they laughed until the tears rolled down their cheeks.

Noah didn't mind. He was used to standing alone and he was used to being laughed at. He didn't care what people thought, so long as he knew what God thought. Now the boat was almost ready. Noah and his three sons led the animals into the ark and his wife and his sons' wives carried in the last of the food: seed for the birds, grain for the cattle and horses, dried fruit for themselves — every kind of food there was, enough to last for a long, long time. When the last chipmunk and caterpillar were in the ark God Himself shut them in. At that, seeing them all aboard a boat on dry land, Noah's noisy neighbors laughed louder than ever.

And while they were laughing, it began to rain.

Day and night, the storm continued. In the pale light of their oil lamps, Noah and his family sat and listened to the terrible rain pounding on the roof. After many days they felt the ark gently rocking, and they knew it was floating on the water.

For forty nights the rain poured down. When at last it stopped and Noah opened the window to look out, there was only water, stretching as far as his eyes could see. Not even the tops of the mountains showed above the water. But perhaps, thought Noah, there is dry land farther ahead, out of sight, And so, as the Bible tells us:

...He sent out a dove to see if it could find dry ground, but the dove found no place to light, and returned to Noah, for the water was still too high. So Noah held out his hand and drew the dove back into the boat. Noah waited a week.
...Noah released the dove again, and this time, towards evening, the bird returned to him with an olive leaf in her beak.

So Noah knew that the waters were slowly going down and that somewhere the top of a tree had appeared. But it was a whole year from the time the rain began until the earth was dry enough to walk on again. Then out of the ark they ran, Noah and his family and all the animals that had been cooped up so long, to stretch their legs on the good earth again. They wanted to skip and run and shout for joy, they were

*...Noah released the dove
again, and this time, towards
evening, the bird returned
to him with an olive leaf
in her beak.*

so glad to get out of the crowded boat. But before
he did anything else, Noah built an altar to God,
and offered Him a solemn prayer of thanks.

And God looked down on His world, and He saw
that of all His people only Noah and his family were
left. "But now," thought God, "these people will be
different. They have seen what happens when men
do not listen to Me. Noah's children will not forget Me."

And at first, they didn't forget. Noah's sons
remembered the great Flood and told their sons
about it. The sons' sons heard about it, but it seemed
like a long time ago. So after a while people began
to forget why their family had lived through the Flood.
They forgot how important it was to listen to God,
and they began to do whatever they wanted to instead.
Once more people decided not to follow God's plan.

It was God's plan for all of Noah's children to have
enough to eat. But they didn't follow God's plan. If a
man was strong, he would take all the wheat from his
neighbor's fields and all the fruit from his trees, and
lock them up in his own storehouse. If other people
starved, why should he care?

When he became very rich the strong man called
himself a ruler and then he not only took the wheat
and fruit that other people had raised, but whole cities
that other people had built, to get the gold that was

They invented many little gods to suit their own plans: a god to help them win wars, a god to make it rain, a god to chase wolves away.

in them. He even took the people who lived in the cities and made them his slaves. Then while his slaves struggled with heavy stones to build a storehouse for his stolen gold, the ruler sat back and decided what city he would take next to get more gold and more slaves.

There was little kindness in the world that Noah's children built. Most men did not care how unhappy other people were, so long as they themselves were getting rich.

As for loving God, by this time most people had forgotten God and His plan altogether. They invented many little gods to suit their own plans: a god to help them win wars, a god to make it rain, a god to chase wolves away.

They even imagined what these gods looked like. One god, they thought, was a bull with wings, another had the body of a cat and the face of a man, another one was supposed to be in the shape of a snake.

And God, watching His people, saw that they were getting more confused all the time. "There is only one God!" He kept trying to tell them. "I am not shaped like a bull or a cat or a snake! You can't see Me with your eyes; you must see Me with your heart. Love Me and you will see Me! Love anyone at all and you will catch a glimpse of me!"

It was no use. Most people were not listening any

more. They had shut their ears to Him for so long
that they did not even recognize God's voice.

The Chosen People

The Chosen People

But, as always, a few men did listen. One of these men was Abraham. Abraham lived in a rich and beautiful city called Haran. But one day he heard God's voice say:

Leave your own country behind you, and your own people, and go to the land I will guide you to.
If you do, I will cause you to become the father of a great nation...and the entire world will be blessed because of you.

Abraham was seventy-five years old when he heard these words but, hard as it was to leave his home, he obeyed God, left Haran, and went into the new land.

For many years Abraham and then his sons and his

grandsons were wandering herdsmen in this new land. And God repeated His promise to Abraham's grandson, Jacob.

And God said to him, "You shall no longer be called Jacob, but Israel. I am God Almighty," the Lord said to him..."a great nation, yes, many nations, many kings shall be among your descendants....And I will pass on to you the land I gave to Abraham and... I will give it to you and to your descendants."

But when Jacob (or Israel) was an old man, there was a great famine in this land, and to find food Israel and his children had to leave and go to a country called Egypt. There they were eventually made slaves. For hundreds of years they worked for the Egyptians. It seemed almost as if God had forgotten His promise that He would make them a great nation. But God never forgets.

Egypt in those days was the richest country in the world: the Pharaoh had more slaves and more gold and more storehouses than any other king. The Pharaoh and all the other Egyptians believed in many different gods and built huge temples for them, thinking that the more temples a god had the more pleased he would be and the more favors he would do for Egypt. But since none of their gods really existed, the great temples were wasted.

To find food Israel and his children had to leave and go to a country called Egypt. There they were eventually made slaves. For hundreds of years they worked for the Egyptians.

The Egyptians forced their slaves to build their temples for them, and as the years went by many of the Israelites forgot God and worshiped the false gods of Egypt. Perhaps a few were true to the one God; we do not know. But they dared not worship Him openly. All day they slaved in the mud pits, making bricks for the temples of the Egyptians. But at night, while the Egyptians were chanting and singing in the great temples, perhaps these few went back to the hovels where they lived, locked their doors, and prayed in whispers to the one true God.

And God heard their prayers. He hears whispers just as clearly as shouts, and He likes hovels as well as palaces.

God needed these humble slaves. Why did He need them? He needed them to entrust with the gift that He was preparing for all mankind. God was getting ready for Christmas, and the gift He was giving the world was so priceless and so rare that He could not place it in unworthy hands.

You see, God had thought of a way to bring His children back to Him — the children He had lost — and this way was Christmas.

It seems strange that He still wanted them back, these people who had disappointed Him so often. They had brought Him little but sorrow ever since

He had created them. He had given them the power to choose, and they had chosen to disobey Him. He had created them to be His friends, and they spent most of their time fighting each other. He had talked with them, and they had turned away. He ought to have been thoroughly tired of them.

But He wasn't. God's patience does not wear out, as man's does. It did not matter what men did or how long they stayed away from Him, He still longed for them as a father longs for a child who has run away.

But God had seen that, by themselves, they would never find their way back to Him. It didn't matter whether He started with Adam or Noah, with bad men or good men; sooner or later people wandered outside His plan and were hopelessly separated from Him.

Have you ever watched a fly trying to go straight through a closed window? It flies at the glass again and again, trying to get into the clear air beyond. The fly doesn't know — but you know — that he will never get past that glass unless you take pity on him and open the window.

That must have been how God felt as He watched men flying at the wall they had built between themselves and Him. "They're never going to get past that wall," God must have said, "unless I open a way for them. They are separated from Me, and this separation is death.

"But what if I were to take away this death that follows sin? What if I sent my Son to take this death for men, so that they would not have to die?"

If it seems to be a cruel answer, we must remember that sin is cruel, that what it does to men is cruel, and that to save us from this death, God had to give the very life of His Son. For Jesus is the way that God opened to us, the way back to fellowship with Him.

But how could the Son of God die? God's Son was One with God Himself. He was not a man. He was Spirit. Like God's, His life had no beginning. How could His life end when it had never begun?

To die, the Son of God would have to be born. This is the gift God was planning. He was going to send His Son to earth as a human baby. He would be born, just as you were, a tiny infant too weak to lift up its head. He would have to learn all the things other babies learn: how to crawl, how to stand, how to run. Later He would be a boy, no faster runner than any other boy in town. He would live in His family's house, help around the home, and obey His parents and teachers.

And then, when He was a man, He would bring men back to the God they had forgotten. He would

tell them why God had made them and put them
on this earth. He would tell them:
The Lord our God is the one and only God. And you
must love Him with all your heart and soul and mind
and strength…and…you must love others as much
as yourself.

He would show them, too, as well as tell them.
In His own life they could see what God meant by
"love." He would feed the hungry and heal the sick
and make the blind see.

And finally He would show them the greatest love
of all: He would die for them, and after that the way
would be opened for all who would to return to God.

After that no matter how a person sinned, no matter
how far from God's plan he wandered, there would
still be this way back. For love like this would be
stronger than sin — stronger than death itself.

This was the gift God was preparing, and this was
why He needed the children of Israel. These humble
slaves were to make a home on earth for His Son.
"There shall come a Star out of Jacob," He said,
"and a Sceptre shall rise out of Israel." Already God
saw the star over Bethlehem and Jesus as Lord of
all mankind.

There was a man in Egypt named Moses. He was
an Israelite by birth, but he had been adopted as a

baby by Pharaoh's daughter and raised as an Egyptian Prince. The Bible tells us he *"chose to share ill-treatment with God's people instead of enjoying the pleasures of sin for a little while."* He was God's man for the tremendous task that lay ahead.

"Come," said God to Moses. "Now I am going to send you to Pharaoh, to demand that he let you lead my people out of Egypt."

Moses knew that Pharaoh would be furious at such a suggestion. After all, why would a king want to let his valuable slaves go free? Then who would build his temples and do the unpleasant chores?

But Moses went to Pharaoh anyway and said, *"The God of Israel...says, 'Let my people go!'"*

As Moses had known he would, the king turned pale with anger. *"Who is the Lord,"* he asked haughtily, *"that I should listen to Him and let Israel go?"* And in his anger, he gave the children of Israel harder work to do.

Then God sent down plagues on Egypt. One of them was a plague of frogs. There were so many frogs that they covered the ground. They were everywhere the Egyptians stepped. They even hopped into their beds and jumped into the dough when the cooks tried to make bread.

The Egyptians prayed to all their gods and offered

God sent down plagues on Egypt. One of them was a plague of frogs. There were so many frogs that they covered the ground. They were everywhere the Egyptians stepped.

them fabulous gifts if they would only take the frogs away. The frogs only grew thicker. Then at last Pharaoh sent for Moses and said, not quite so haughtily,

"Plead with God to take the frogs away, and I will let the people go and sacrifice to Him."

But Pharaoh was lying, for when God had taken the frogs away, he only laughed at Moses and would not keep his promise.

Then more plagues came to the Egyptians: lice, flies, boils, hail, locusts — and at last, the most dreadful of all — the death of the first born of men and animals. Now, in terror, the king begged Moses to take his people and leave Egypt at once.

The children of Israel grabbed their belongings and hurried out of Egypt as fast as they could, praising God for setting them free. But once more Pharaoh had tricked them. While they were resting from their fast march at the edge of a sea, they heard the sound of horses' hoofs in the distance. The sound came closer and now they could hear the chariot wheels, too. Pharaoh and his army were coming after them.

They were trapped, with the sea in front of them and Pharaoh closing in behind them!

The children of Israel cried to Moses, saying they should have stayed in Egypt.

"It would be better to be slaves to the Egyptians

than dead in the wilderness."

But Moses said to them, *"Don't be afraid. Just stand where you are and watch, and you will see the wonderful way the Lord will rescue you today. The Egyptians you are looking at — you will never see them again."*

And then with a mighty wind God blew back the water of the sea until there was a dry path through the middle of it and the children of Israel marched across to the other side on dry land. The chariots were close behind them. The Egyptians thundered into the dry path, too, their spears and arrows gleaming. But as the children of Israel reached the other side, the water closed in and Pharaoh's army was never seen again.

At last the children of Israel were free to worship the one true God. On a mountaintop there on the other side of the sea, God gave Moses the Ten Commandments and the other laws that His chosen people were to live by.

Then He led them into the land He had promised them. In those days it was called Canaan, but today it is known as the Holy Land because it was the home God chose for His Son.

Moses was an old man when the children of Israel reached Canaan, and he did not live to see them settled in their new land. But God spoke to His people through other men. One of them was a man named Isaiah and through Isaiah God told His people about the Savior who was coming:

The people who walk in darkness shall see a great Light — a Light that will shine on all those who live in the land of the shadow of death.

For unto us a Child is born; unto us a Son is given; and the government shall be upon his shoulders. These will be his royal titles: "Wonderful Counselor," "The Mighty God," "The Everlasting Father," "The Prince of Peace."

Where was this child to be born? Through a man named Micah, God gave the answer:

O Bethlehem...you are but a small Judean village, yet you will be the birthplace of my King who is alive from everlasting ages past.

God had chosen the people and the place. Now He had to choose the right time.

The Time Grows Short

The Time Grows Short

It had to be a very special time — the time when God's Son came into the world. It had to be a time when many people could understand one language. After His Son had done His great work of love, of course God would want people everywhere to know about it. He would want them to know that death was finished, that the long separation was over, that they could come back into that close fellowship with Him whenever they chose to, that sin could never again build an everlasting wall between them and God.

How was this wonderful news going to get to every person in the world? At first only the children of Israel would know about it.

Joseph. Long ago a man named Jeremiah had told the children of Israel that the Savior, when He came, would belong to the family of David, and both Mary and Joseph were members of that family, descended from the great King David. Joseph took good care of Mary as the time grew near for her Baby to be born.

But what about the words of Micah who had said that the Savior would be born in Bethlehem? Nazareth, where Joseph and Mary lived, was almost a hundred miles from Bethlehem by the twisting road, and in those days a hundred miles was a tremendous distance. But, as we shall see, Micah was right.

The emperor in Rome at that time was Caesar Augustus. That meant "Caesar the Splendid," and although the people didn't think he was splendid everybody in the world obeyed the emperor. But how many people was "everybody in the world"? Caesar didn't know.

So he decided to count them. Of course, he didn't want to count them just so that he could say, "Well, well. I am emperor of twenty million" (or however many it was). He wanted to know how many people he ruled so that he would know how much gold they could pay to him.

Each year every country in his empire had to send him a certain amount of gold as taxes. If it had no gold, the country had to send him its fattest sheep or a whole camel-train of its finest wheat. Of course, a large country had to give more to Caesar than a small country. So, in order to know how much each country should pay, Caesar had to count all the people in the world.

Now, in order to keep the different families and places in the huge empire straight, Caesar decided that everyone should go back to the town where his family had first lived, to be taxed there.

And when Caesar Augustus decided something, it was the law. All over the Roman world people had to go to their home towns and be counted for the tax. It might not be convenient to go. A farmer might be planting his wheat just then. It might not even be safe. There might be old people in a family, or a very young baby, or perhaps a sick person. But when Caesar said, "Go!" — people went.

Do you remember how it began, the story we heard on Christmas morning?

About this time Caesar Augustus, the Roman Emperor, decreed that a census should be taken throughout the nation....Everyone was required to return to his ancestral home for this registration. And because Joseph was a member of the royal line, he had to go to Bethlehem in Judea, King David's ancient

home — journeying there from the Galilean village
of Nazareth. He took with him Mary, his fiancee,
who was obviously expecting a child by this time.

Now is the time. Now is the very year and the very day. This is the time for the Son of God to be born.

The First Christmas

The First Christmas

f all the times in the world to live, imagine living then! What if we had been alive on that very day! What if we had lived not only at the very time but had been in the very town where Jesus was born!

Nobody can choose when he will live. You and I were born nearly two thousand years after that first Christmas day, and had nothing to say about it. But there's nothing to stop us from pretending — just as we have been pretending that you are visiting us in our home and sleeping on the trundle bed in our guest room.

What if, instead of living in the twentieth century, we had lived in Bethlehem just as the first century began, and you had been our guest there? If you can imagine yourself up on the top of our mountain, you can imagine yourself over the ocean to Bethlehem. Then — but this is harder — you can imagine yourself back through time. Back through all those years. Back to the day when your bed was a blanket on the floor, when traveling by camel-back was the best way to get anywhere, and when Caesar Augustus was the ruler of the world.

Let's pretend that we lived in a little house in Bethlehem and you and your family were among the many descendants of David who had come to Bethlehem to be taxed. You might very well have stayed in our house. Bethlehem had only one small inn and that had been filled by the first travelers to arrive, so the rest had to find a place to sleep in the houses of strangers, or in stables or wherever there was room to lie down.

In that way, that first Christmas in Bethlehem would have been like our Christmas today. Our house would have been full of guests then, too, both grownups and children. But it wouldn't have been a happy get-together as it is today. It was no holiday then. Families were coming to Bethlehem to pay taxes to an emperor they hated. They came in fear and anger. They didn't know, you see, that Christmas was about to happen.

And of course we couldn't have offered you a
trundle bed to sleep in — in those days ordinary
people didn't have beds. Everybody carried his own
sleeping-blanket with him. During the day he wrapped
it about him as a cloak and at night he simply spread
it out on the floor and lay down on it. But at least
that made it easy to have guests. There was no counting
noses to make sure there were enough beds to go
around. A Bethlehem family could have as much
company as it had floor space.

There would have been no fireplace in our home
either; in Bethlehem people didn't use fireplaces.
And we probably wouldn't have eaten at a table.
We would have sat on mats on the floor and held
our meat and bread in our hands — and I'm sure
you children would have found that a more sensible
arrangement. Of course we wouldn't have had oyster
stew for breakfast, or at any other meal. The children
of Israel didn't eat oysters.

What would our names have been? Not Virginia
or Franklin or Nelson Edman, but Bunny and I could
still have been Ruth; Ann might have been Anna, and
we certainly could have had a dog named Belshazzar.

There wouldn't have been much time to play with
him, though, for we would all have been very busy.
I expect I would have spent most of the morning

turning the heavy grinding stone that women used in those days when they had to make their own flour and couldn't buy it in a sack at the grocery store.

In those days, too, all children were expected to help with the work. You boys would have gone with the men to the wheat fields outside the village. And the girls would have gone with me to fill our water jars at the public well down the street. We'd have balanced the big jars on our heads and stepped out cautiously into the narrow, crowded street.

Bethlehem was so crowded with travelers then that it must have been hard to move through the streets. Men tugged and shouted at heavy-laden donkeys, women carried tiny children, older children lugged bundles of food. The people in the streets looked cross and tired. Some of them were headed for the large house where the Roman soldiers were taking names for the tax rolls. Others had just arrived in Bethlehem and were peering anxiously into the crowded doorways, wondering where they would find a place to spend the night. All they needed was room enough to spread out their cloaks and a little water to wash the dust of travel from their feet, but even those simple things were hard to find then.

We would have edged along the crowds in the street, hoping no one would jostle us. Coming back would have been even slower, because the jars would be heavy. But when at last all the jars were filled, and the men's work in the fields was finished, I think I know where you would have gone. I think you would have headed for the gate where the north road came into Bethlehem. You would have climbed up onto the sun-warmed stone wall and sat down beside the other children and the old men to watch the latest strangers coming into town.

Here came a whole family: four children, the mother and father, the grandmother, and that very old woman on the donkey must be the great-grandmother. They looked tired as they trudged up this last hill. Probably they looked forward to a comfortable place to stay. You wished there were more room in our house.

Alone and in groups the people came, walking rapidly on this last bit of their journey, up the hill to Bethlehem. Some of them, the old men said, were coming from as far away as the town of Nazareth. You could hardly believe it. Almost a hundred miles! That meant three or four nights sleeping beside the road.

That man coming now, down in the valley, must be rich; he rode a camel! Not even his gold would buy him a room in Bethlehem tonight, you thought. You turned to the old man sitting beside you on the wall and, because old men knew everything, you asked him, "Why do all these people have to come to Bethlehem to be counted?"

The old man closed his eyes as if he were looking back over hundreds of years. "Their great-great-great-great-grandfathers once lived here," he said at last. "That makes this their home town, too, just as it's ours. And Caesar" — the old man leaned forward and spat on the road to show what he thought of Caesar — "Caesar doesn't care how far people have to travel if it makes his bookkeeping a little easier." The old man's eyes glared with anger.

The camel was lurching past you now. The rich rider's eyes were angry, too — angry and a little sad. It was the look in the eyes of all the travelers coming into Bethlehem. They didn't like having to make this trip, and they didn't like having to pay taxes to Rome. But what could they do? That was the way the world was. The strong took from the weak, the man with the sword made the laws, no one loved anyone but himself. It had always been that way, and always would be. There was nothing you could do to change it.

The afternoon sun was hot on your back. The wall was warm. For a minute, your eyes closed. When they opened, two people were coming along the dusty road down in the valley, a man walking and a woman riding

Two people were coming along the dusty road down in the valley, a man walking and a woman riding a donkey.

a donkey. But how slowly these two were coming. The woman had her hand on the man's shoulder and she seemed very weary. The man kept looking at her anxiously.

Two men walking rapidly with tall staffs passed the couple and the donkey, climbed the hill, and went in through the town gate. Now the man and woman had reached the hill and you could see the donkey was covered with dust, as if he had come a long way. Why were they stopping so often, now that their trip was almost over? They stopped again, right in front of you. The woman turned to look at the man and as she did you saw her face. You saw it and your heart gave a little leap.

For on this young woman's face, so pale and travel-weary, was a smile that made you forget taxes and Roman soldiers and even Caesar Augustus himself. In hot, noisy, crowded Bethlehem, her smile seemed to say that all the joy of heaven had come down to earth.

That night, wrapped up in your cloak on the crowded floor of your house, you could not get to sleep for thinking of her smile. It was an unusual thing, these days, to see a happy face. You wondered if the man and woman had found a place to sleep.

Why was she so happy? And you, why were you

yourself so wide-awake and excited tonight? Was it the thought of that smile that made you want to get up and dance and shout and run through the streets? You didn't do it, of course. You lay still, still as a log, so that you wouldn't wake your mother and father who were squeezed up against you on the crowded floor. But a few feet away you saw one of the other children lift his head, and you knew that he was not asleep either. None of the children who had seen Mary were asleep that night.

This was a special night. You didn't know how you knew it, but you knew that something wonderful was about to happen to you. To you and to everyone. Something so wonderful you were almost afraid to breathe for fear of breaking the stillness.

For tonight Bethlehem was very still. On other nights donkeys coughed in their stables and wolves howled from their hill tops. But on this most special of all nights, even the donkeys and the wolves were quiet. The wind itself stopped blowing. The animals and the sky and a few wide-awake children were quiet. Listening. Waiting for something.

It was very late in the night when you suddenly jumped up from the floor. In an instant the other children were on their feet. There was a commotion out in the street. You could hear men shouting, running, their sandals scuffing on the rough stones of the street. You ran to the door, stepping over sleeping grown-ups wrapped in their cloaks.

You stared at these men who were talking so loudly in the middle of the night. They looked like country men, sheepherders. What was it they were saying? They had seen an angel!

You looked at them again to make sure they were really shepherds and not lunatics. No, they were tough-looking surely, but not crazy — strong men who lived out of doors and fought wolves from their sheep with nothing but a few sticks and stones. They were not the kind of men who would be imagining things.

They had seen an angel, they repeated. And the angel had told them about a Baby born in Bethlehem and called the Baby "Savior" and "Lord." They had just seen the Baby with their own eyes — out in the stable behind the inn — and they wanted everyone else to know about it, too.

You didn't wait to hear any more. All of you children set off down the street as fast as you could run, past houses where sleepy people were stumbling to the doors, asking what all the racket was about. To the inn, then around it to the stable, then, slowly, softly, in at the door.

There she was. The young woman with the radiant

smile. She was leaning against one of the stalls, and the eyes in the happy face were closed. The man was at her side. And behind them, in the manger where the cows came for their food, was the Baby.

He was a tiny thing, wrapped tightly in a long linen band of cloth and sleeping as soundly as any newborn baby. Sleeping as though the world had not waited thousands of years for this moment. As soundly as though your life and my life and the life of everyone on earth were not wrapped up in His birth. As though from this moment on all the sin and sorrow of the world were not His problem.

Should you speak to His mother resting so quietly there? Should you ask her if you might touch the Baby — not to wake Him, but just to touch His hand?

What a moment that would have been! To have reached out your own hand and touched the Son of God!

There she was. The young woman with the radiant smile. He was a tiny thing...sleeping as soundly as any newborn baby.

*A*nd yet — do you know — I don't really envy those people, who might have been you and me. I don't envy the people who lived in Bethlehem that night, even though many of them must have seen Jesus and Mary and Joseph with their own eyes. For they couldn't have known all that they were seeing.

They couldn't know all that this Baby was born to do: the words of joy He would speak to an unhappy world, the love He would show to people too used to hatred, the victory He would win over the sin and sorrow of the world.

You and I are greatly blessed to live now, when His work of love is finished. He is as close to us today as He was to the children of Bethlehem. Closer, for today we do not even have to reach out our hands to touch Him.

If we are really sorry for our sins, we can come to Him just as truly as those shepherds did in Bethlehem. And He will forgive us and give back to us that joyous fellowship with God — lost so long ago in the Garden of Eden. This is the Christmas gift that God gives to me and to everyone on earth.

And if, on Christmas morning, when the presents are opened and the fire is burning low, we want to go back to Bethlehem, then we have only to open our

Bible to the second chapter of the Book of Luke, knowing who this man and this woman are, coming up the hill to Bethlehem. Knowing why they have come and why the angels sing. Knowing the meaning of what we read:

And while they were there, the time came for her baby to be born; and she gave birth to her first child, a son. She wrapped him in a blanket and laid him in a manger, because there was no room for them in the village inn.

That night some shepherds were in the fields outside the village, guarding their flocks of sheep. Suddenly an angel appeared among them, and the glory of the Lord shone all around them. They were badly fright-ened, but the angel reassured them. "Don't be afraid!" he said. "I bring you the most joyful news ever an-nounced, and it is for everyone! The Savior — yes, the Messiah, the Lord — has been born tonight in Bethlehem! How will you recognize Him? You will find a Baby wrapped in a blanket, lying in a manger!" Suddenly, the angel was joined by a vast host of others — praising God: "Glory to God in the highest heaven," they sang, "and peace on earth, good will to all men."

BIBLE REFERENCES

Luke 2:1-12 / 18,19
Genesis 2:17 / 35
Genesis 3:1-5;10-13 / 35
Genesis 3:14 / 40
Genesis 6:5-6;14,16 / 48
Genesis 8:8-11 / 51
Genesis 12:1-3 / 58
Genesis 35:10-11 / 59
Mark 13:30-31 / 64
Hebrews 11:25 / 64
Exodus 3:10 / 65
Exodus 5:1-2 / 65
Exodus 8:8 / 67
Exodus 14:12-13 / 67,68
Isaiah 9:2,6 / 69
Micah 5:2 / 69
Luke 1:30-31 / 75
Luke 2:1-5 / 78,79
Luke 2:6-14 / 95